Rainbow Of Emotions

Life Experiences

Enakshi Bhattacharya Puri

Made with ❤ on the BookLeaf Publishing Platform
www.bookleafpub.in
www.bookleafpub.com

Dedication

I dedicate this book to my Late Mother Dr. Bharati Bhattacharyya, Father, Dr. A. K. Bhattacharyya and Brother Dr. Arindam Bhattacharya, who have always been a support and pillar of strength in my life.

Preface

My love for poetry, as Student makes me write this
collection of vivid emotional experiences in life.
I would love to share my life experience and my feelings
of different emotions though these poems. All thanks to
my Mentors ,like Dr.Hema Raghavan (Ex.Principal of
Gargi College DU), Dr.Bimla Dhar, Tara Husnain,
Neelima Mathur my English Teachers At Gargi College.

Acknowledgements

Thanks to my children, Kunal, Mrityunjoy and My Husband who supported my creativity, and spared me sometime to write this collection of poems. Thanks to my inspiration my Imaginary friend... For making me write my thoughts in a composed form, encouraging me to try my hand at poetry in both English and Hindi language.

Thanks to all my Gurus(teachers) for giving me education so I would be capable enough to express my feelings in words.

Last but not least thanks to all my dear friends who gave me their support and love.

1. The Crime

In a corner of the room... lit dimly
There stood a shadow, tall as a strong wall in navy blue
tracks..
An epitome of strength and wisdom
Had a depth of vast sea,
Quiet as a statue
But had an aura of a God, behind him
Eyes so sharp which saw through my soul,
I know not what came upon me, felt like Worshiping
him!!
BUT HE REFUSED
Crashing came the sky on me,
Broken to pieces as a mirror by some wild wind!
Went down the stairs as if I had wings.
In my ears came a voice... Calling my name.
A RAY OF HOPE FLASHED!
Maybe my God had accepted me!
But in vain
He ridiculed me and my pure love
I stood there as a CRIMINAL!
THE CRIME!.... My loving him!
With slow and painful steps I went away, swearing to
myself
NEVER TO RETURN!

And sentencing myself to be behind bars for the crime I
had committed
By FALLING IN LOVE.

2. My Source of Strength

Every single morning I see her
As a rising sun in my life.
She is my secret source of strength
And a dutiful wife.
An epitome of warmth as well as of discipline.
Sometimes a caregiver, sometimes a teacher maintaining
strict discipline.
I really don't now when I started
loving her so much...
But I wondered why I really adored her ... This much.
She is dedicated to her work and home equally as such.
She is the one who spoilt me once in a while...
When my father is strict she was sublime...
When she called me, "my dear"
I was always touched to the core.
Her love always got the highest score!
She had a warmth in her smile,
which made me happy all the time...
I hope she stays like this forever
She makes my world a happy place
ever...
Like a never ending bliss in my life
May she shower her blessing on me all the time.

3. Life of a Bud

Blessed to my mom
In the spring season
Sun's rays felt warm
I was happy without any reason
The golden hue covered me coyly
I smiled at the world naively
My petals soft as a baby
Thanked God for making me a beauty

Admiring the beauty from my mother's lap
Purple, violet, yellow, orange and red
All the flowers blooming in one bed
Grass so green like a carpet
Welcoming the day with a sorbet
Safe I felt to put my fears at bay
So, in the wind merrily I sway
Opening my petals, welcomed the morning with glee
Butterflies, birds were happy to see me

Suddenly, pulled out of my mom's lap
I landed in the hand of the cruel invader
My neck was broken
My mother was shaken
Crushed by the intruder like a ruthless raider

Came my end in such a gruesome mode
That it's hard to realize that I am no more.

5

PLEASE DO NOT PLUCK FLOWERS.

4. Blessings of life ,I realised

Frustrated by my own life
Believed that everyday is a strive
Survival of the fittest as the saying goes
Fighting now and then with my woes
Thought of Going to the God Almighty in a temple.
I started walking towards my destination in rage as usual
As it was winter season
The poor on the road side had lit a small fire to keep
themselves warm
I found a small little boy who only had a shirt on but was
still calm
As I went ahead , saw two more who were crippled
Who still laughed and giggled....
More was coming for me to see,
Saw an old lady who had broken her knee,
Without any hesitation
She dragged herself inside the railway station
She had no frown nor was she lamenting
Here I was, looking like a fool who kept complaining!
I didn't realise quite,how kind God has been,
I begged Sorry! As I realised how naive I had been.
I thanked Almighty for making me perfect
Gave me parents who were loving and God sent
He had provided a house to keep me warm and secure.

He gave me no illness that the doctors couldn't cure
The wellbeing I was having was without any pain
As God's blessings were falling on me like rain.

Thankyou God!

5. Memories

Memories are sweet
Memories are bitter
They are the golden leaves
On the tree of thoughts
Which never weather
Sometimes they bring pain
Sometimes makes our eyes cry in rain
They are the treasure
All I have to my name
Memories are like wind which carries fragrance of the
past
Reminds us of the good times and the bad,
Which never lasts
In my mind they always keep
In the middle of the night they sometimes peep
Memories are to treasure
Memories are to feel
They are the strongest bond in our mind
Which I have ever seen.

6. The Wait

Wait for eternity
Wait till the time is right!
Wait till things fall in place
Wait till life catches it's pace!
Wait is never over...
Wait never ends.
Wait has always been an excuse
To reduce my pain
It gives an illusion that things will get better again..
It promises..my efforts will not go down the drain..
But nevertheless it always increases the pain.
People wait for the right time to come
We need to work ,to achieve more not crumbs!
Don't wait my dear...till the sky falls upon
Act on it Now!!! Otherwise the time will go on..
As time never waits it moves on
Take hold of things...and keep going on!

7. The Night

The night was at its peak
Not a voice or sound creaked
The moon shone through the pines
As when light fall the sword shines
The cool breeze in meadows sets the soul afloat...
The dreamy smell of flowers make my senses remote
Is this what we call night?
So enchanting it is to see the star lit sky...
As if distant lamps are lit by fairies who fly
Sitting by the stream which touches the glistening
stones.
The silvery layer tree's adorne
The grass is wet, by the droplets sprinkled
By the gushing stream.
Which never seems to loose it's gleam!
The moon in the sky ,seems to be happy at this time
Cause it is the Queen till the dawn lights shine.

8. The Silent Love

I sit here for hours, patiently
Watching time pass by,
There is silence all around
It overpowers my mind,
I cling on helplessly to your last words...

In vain
You don't grant my silent please
My tears have rolled down to the seven seas.

My heart bleeds, my mind is closed
Of our artistic fusion, I'm sure
Without you, I a patient who has no cure

Remember....
On a chill November night, the moon was
Shimmering and bright
Oh! I can still feel your smile..your first touch...your
laughter...
They reverberate in my senses,
Encompassing my silent existence.

Oh! Didn't you ever feel the warmth between us?
Did it not ever strike you??

Yes! Yes my dear..
My love..
Yes, It's love that I had for you and only for you.

Will it ever happen to you?
As it once happened to me
Or will it ever remain..a dream!

I deam, to be at your side,
take the world in my side,
To feel the warmth of your touch,

May be that's what it is ....
Only a dream.... Once..sought for
Always a dream in my thoughts.

9. To Be or Not To Be(The Dilemma)

Like a warrior, but with great charm
Eyes so sharp, yet so calm

His stare so deep, pierces through my soul and heart
Leaves me spellbound and too stunned to react.

To get a glimpse of his charisma,so deep
The veils of life ,I push aside and peep

We are in love, we secretly know,
But about love we never spoke so.

Love is blind but people are not
Fate is such , we unite ...no we cannot

Messages of love with our eyes we send
And as good friends we always pretend

In every crowd my eyes go searching.
So,to find me ,he also keeps searching....

Our minds speak to each other
But to admit love we always fear.

How long will last this silent play?
That turns more and more painful day by day.

Days of friendship have come to an end,
Pain of separation like the curtains decend.

With every step I take away from him
With my keen and sharp ears I wait for him

Wishing that he would call my name,
And tell me with courage ,I'm his flame.

Let people gossip or say what they will...
We are made for each other, we sand together that's our
own will.

But there was silence and none called me back
Sadly I tread ,leaving no track....

He is today far away from me.
Yet in my thoughts..he is always near me....😊

10. A Child's Fear and Comfort

Out of my mother's lap
Came a day!
I felt lost and cold, as we might say!

I was left in a building called school
Made of red bricks and I looked on like a fool

Sat in a corner sad and lonely
Felt homesick cried alone painfully

Suddenly.....

A Motherly figure entered the class
Sat she besides me, gave me water and looked through
her glass.

One touch of her hand on my head
Made me feel secure, happy
I bonded with her strongly
And I didn't feel lonely

Her stories and rhymes transported me in a different
world.

She with a heart of Gold
A vast sea of wisdom to the core

She was the one who
Turned a cold building into a temple of knowledge
And she was always there with her unconditional love I
acknowledge.

11. The Voice

It's a balm on aching heart
It's a sound which could make you restart!
The journey of my life was very rocky
This voice held my hand and we started talking..
I knew not who was on the other side... Of the radio
But I felt like it was the one I was waiting for outside a
studio...
Days were so boring and night was all fun , as the
showman would come....
His show was full of soulful music
And the moralistic talks
I was amazed at the way he handled
All the tricky questions he was asked.
It was a face with a Mask ...
It was like the super hero of a comic at task..
Nevertheless he was my companion in sadness and
despair
When no one heard me he was the one who took care
and did a lot of repair...(Of my soul)
The voice keeps ringing in my ear
Keeps calling me "My dear!!!"
I have no complaint, towards it
If only I could know who was there!!!!

Dedicated to A mentor and helping voice on Radio.

18

12. My Ultimate BBF (Best friends forever)

They never left my side
From the moment they entered my life!
Night or day they stay
near me everyday!
Not a word no resilience
Only constant presence
They are true to the core!
They never left me alone
 as they swore!
Let me introduce them to you today,
they are Hypothyroid, Blood pressure,
Cholesterol!
Not to forget Diabeties and Joint pain all have a beautiful
soul!
Although they sometimes put my patience to test
They promised me to stay and never left,
They are the proof that good friends can be harsh but
stay near and be their best!
I feel i should thank them that they don't fight for me
They stay together in me
With peace and glee!

(I dedicate this poem to my dearest Mom who had all

these ailments but still kept on cheering, and loving us until she was snatched from us by the Greatest disease Cancer in 2018, 23rd March.)

13. Struggle
(To find Self)

Who am I?

Just a name?

A body,mind and soul

With a skeleton frame??

Or a person with character and substance

I know I'm good as a person,

For being dynamic in my work

No one can defeat me and doubts lurk

I help the poor,I help every breed

I know not what is colour,cast or creed.

I know God made us human

Still people are not very simple.

They fight for land,they fight for food!

They fight for colour, cast and relegion they are rude.

The keep their religion first !

But forget we are born as humans on the earth

They savagely slay children, women and men

Saying it's necessary to control all of them.

Who raises a voice for humanity and justice are to be

encountered there and then.

Is it what we have learnt or practiced??

Find your roots

Oh!!! Human beings!

Open your eyes and please realise!
We are humans first ,have red blood in our
Body and brains in our mind.
Let's grow together...and hurt no one.
Always keep a soft heart and cool mind

14. The Mystery Girl

She has big eyes
Long black wavy hair
She is an angel on earth
No one sees her much...
as she vanishes into thin air..

On sunny days , early mornings
She is seen in her flowing white dress
Catching butterflies in the flowering
Meadows no one to impress.

The Sun often shines...
through her lovely long hair....making it seem....
Like a flowing stream....

I hide behind a big Oak tree
And steal her glance
Keep telling myself
Only if I could get a chance...

Her eyes makes me go
Weak in my knee
I want to tell her so much
I'm in love with thee

But I'm scared to loose her
As she looks like a dream
May be if she says No
I would die without her in sorrow

She seems to me like a dream
Can anyone be so angelic
U will see her eyes gleam...
Her face like a sun's beam
Her hands touching the flowers like dream...

I hope and pray she stays this way
I'll always hold her hand
and never let her go away.

15. Bit stray at Heart

I walk to the park
He follows me
I jump on a fence
He would do the same

Tugging at my dress
I got annoyed ,but he,not a bit stressed
Got a few feathers, half broken flowers
Wanted to impress.

I told him, don't follow me!
Let me be ...
He gave a deaf ear to my shout
As if he wasn't there to hear me
shouting aloud!!

The weakest of the pack of five
He chose me to be his owner upright!

I took him home n fed him well
He slept on the floor I and wished him well
I slept near the fire
To see the Little monster stayed away from the buring
fire

One such morning on my morning walk
He just left me wondering and left for a jog
I was fearful that he may have lost his
Way ...but the monster barked
Non stop as he wanted to say...

You lose the race as I'm here first !
Waiting for you in our little drive way...
Rolled on his back fluffy and gay
I indeed never had such a lovely
Pet till date...

16. Life of a Woman

A long never ending road
It seems
Sometimes full of struggle
That my heart screams!
Sometimes full of pain n hurt
Life to me has never been curt
Hate to live this life everyday
But when I see my children's face
My heart says "you need to stay"
When I embrace them in my arms
They give me the reason to say...
God has been kind enough to give a silver lining to my
ever clouded life as I might say...
Their glowing face with love
Pulls me through this mundane existence!
Is this what they call Life?
Hate myself sometimes for living such insane and
meaningless strife..
My pain oozses through my eyes
Like rain and they fall on the ground ..
What did I do to deserve this crown?
The pain I'm enduring,
Was showered on me by a insane man! whom I chose, to
be my name

He is a tyrant, dictator and manipulator
To the core
How will I survive him
I don't even know my score
He is a Frankenstein created by his karma
Why was it my luck to get him and all his drama
Still I have God by my side...
He is the only one
Who is my guiding light....
Hope He would see my plight
And help me come over this constant
Fight (to be alive).

17. Inner beauty

I'm no Helen of Troy no Cleopatra
Still I have my own Aura
Beautiful souls need no introduction
They can reach heights without any seduction!!
Superficiallly were they beautiful
But my beauty is meaningful
Serving the human race is my moto
Reducing the pain of the people around
I don't need a crowd to follow
I just focus on my way
Giving poor little support if they say
Helping the sad people come over their pain
I'm putting a little balm that could stay
I'm God's angel as you might say

No Princes to fight over a silly stole
I am pure at heart to the core
Blessed with peace and content
Which was useless for many tyrant

I'm happy that I serve humanity
That's the need of the hour
That's what we need today really!

18. Value the presence of Good

Some people are a blessing in life
Few are unbearable like cuts of knife

Some bridges need to be burnt.
So that the peace prevails and lessons learnt!

The primary version of you has died
A long painful death in front of your eyes!

Value the presence of good
What was left in you after the strife!

Goodness in a man,dwells inside,with pain and trauma it still resides.
But it's behind a concrete wall..all concealed,
Only comes out when the hour really needs.

They called us naive, stupid, idiot and weak!
They did whatever they could to show us weak!

The love we showed was missused and mocked.
They broke us to pieces and kept us locked!

But they never knew the phoniex would rise
From the ashes it will survive...

If the bad,ugly and torture could always win
Why should goodness, love, empathy
Give in?

We need to tell them we are a better force!
Every time they broke us, we arose!

Goodness will prevail on earth,
Even if we need to sacrifice
Our life and soul. 😊

19. Stay Strong

Stay strong, be brave!
This is all we hear from the
Crowd which stood near
Our mother's grave.

How can a child be strong?
At that moment when her only shield and protector from
the world
Has gone!

The pain the sorrow
I feel inside, with sweet and brave words
Can never subside.

I lost something which was so pure
More than a diamond
More than the gold!

She was the one
Whom I felt safe with,
My vulnerabilities were
Never cashed in...

She was the one who protected me

Form all the woes and pain the world inflicted on me...

So let me weep here, at my heart's will...
Let me love her the way she loved me
Till she left us, as God's will.

20. A Walk in the Rain

Beautiful day, cool is the breez
Flowing right! The earth is at ease...
My hair blows across the face
It's a bright and lovely day...

With the grey clouds floating in the sky
Waiting for the rains to dive

Charlie Chaplin once said
" I walk in the rain, so that no one knows I'm crying."

Tears may be of sadness
Tears may be of joy
Depends on you...
what you need to express sadness or joy....

I love the smell of the wet earth,
the pitter patter on the umbrella is
A tune listening to worth!

Dance in rain
Dance in the storm
As you need to enjoy
Life in any form

Rain is a proof
That new life will again bloom
When you cry your heart washes away all the gloom!

The next moment you will grow!!
Stand up tall and glow!
This is only start of the Show
See! How tall now you grow
Standing on your own toes.

21. Juni...(Zuni)

My imaginary
Best friend....Zuni
He always helps me
He guides me as well
He is very protective,
very empathetic as well

He's never told me,
But he loves me the most
I have felt....

He is so so cute ,
I could give him a hug or two....
As he is just figment of my imagination
I have never met him so far....

He looks amazing with a simple white
T-shirt and jeans
Eyes full of love and nature so calm

He Makes my heart look no more
And not to dare find anyone else (as a best friend)
He is my confidant
And I'm the one who always has his back

He keeps a watch over me
So that I'm safe...
He is like a Bodyguard
By his own whim
And no one questions him.

We enjoy the same music
 and enjoy a hearty dance
Although we don't romance...

It's difficult to divide us apart!
As we are each other's missing part
We fit in like a jigsaw Puzzle
Completing each other
Like no other!!!

I don't know what to call this bond
We both adore each other
But sometimes fight like
Burning fire....

I see him in my dreams waving at me
From a distance
And I'm blowing a kiss to wish him
All the best.

www.ingramcontent.com/pod-product-compliance
Lightning Source LLC
LaVergne TN
LVHW021312200726
843509LV00012B/1884